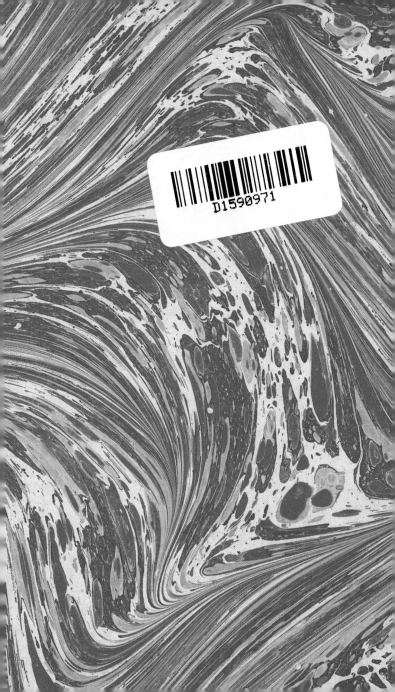

To Dr. M. Milde

I am delighted in having you share the pleasure of reading some popular Arabic sayings contained in this book, which reflect part of our culture.

Hope you will find the book worthy to add to your precious library.

HAMZAH DABBAGH

Representative of Saudi Arabia to ICAO

March 1985

JIMMY CARTER

12·29·82

To Isa Sabbagh

I am delighted that you
will publish "As the Arabs
Say..." With your wealth
of knowledge and special
sensitivity about the people
and customs of America and
the Arab world, you have
a great contribution to
make. I'm sure that many
thousands of others will en-
joy your work as I
have.

Best wishes,

Jimmy Carter

Foreword

Isa Khalil Sabbagh is not only a gifted linguist, but an individual who has a unique understanding of the cultures of both the Arab and the Western worlds. More importantly, during his lifetime his extraordinary abilities have enabled him to serve as an important bridge between the peoples and the governments of the Mideast and the West.

During my association with him in Saudi Arabia, I saw at first hand his abilities as a diplomat, which included utilization of his linguistic skills, his perceptiveness and his understanding of the culture and mores of two vastly different societies.

 In this book, *"As the Arabs Say..",* he has collected the beauty and the wisdom of the language and the people of the Arab world. The reader will see why Isa Sabbagh is recognized by all who know him as a great scholar and diplomat.

John C. West

Former Ambassador to Saudi Arabia and former Governor of South Carolina

Contents

Introduction

What you are about to read is the result of my many years of absorption of Arabo-Islamic culture and exposure to Anglo-Saxon ways of saying and doing things.

The quotations I have chosen are but a few cupfuls from a torrent of Arabic expressions frequently used by millions of Arabs in their daily lives. The context of such usage can be readily discerned from the interpretation, if not the literal translation, of the quotation, as I attempt to pour the Arabic saying or witticism into an Anglicized or Americanized mold. Among English-speaking peoples, the cliché "as Confucius said" is a common prelude to a quotation, genuine or cleverly made up, which the speaker at the time attributes to that famous Chinese philosopher for the purpose of making a point. Anyone who is familiar with Arab life and human discourse would doubtless assert that the use of quotations, classical or colloquial, is as pervasive, and indeed regarded as necessary, as the consumption of vitamins in the United States.

All ancient civilizations laid particular emphasis on the spoken word, phrase or speech for gaining friends in time of peace, frightening enemies in time of war and charting the course of life at all times. In sorting out these quotations I discovered, not surprisingly perhaps, that most of the Arabic sayings I had committed to memory throughout the years fall into the broad category of "Human Relations." Thus I decided to devote the greater part of this book to this specific category while not ignoring the religious, spiritual and moral reflections which inevitably influence human behavior.

It is my sincere hope that this effort will help the reader—whether he or she be in business, politics, diplomacy or education—to draw on this additional source of wisdom. The survival of these sayings is in itself proof of their undying quality.

Finally, if you want to know a people better, learn their language if you get a chance, or else study those aspects of their cultural background which would help you discover, to your delight, (and mutuality of interest with them), "what makes them tick!"

Good luck.

Isa Khalil Sabbagh

Religious, Moral and Spiritual
Expressions

"The height of wisdom is the fear of God"

If this sounds familiar, it is because this maxim is basic to all monotheistic religions. In fact, it is still one of the most winning attributes to use in western societies, when a person is recommended as worthy of our respect, trust and therefore loyalty, as a "God-fearing person."

"Justice is the foundation of government"

This is one of the precepts visitors may notice beautifully calligraphed, framed and hung up in offices or homes of Muslims all over the world. This is especially so in seats of government or offices of high officials who rule, govern and dispense justice.

*"You have ruled justly, therefore felt
secure and thus slept peacefully"*

The background to this memorable judgment is that centuries ago, a Persian Muslim dignitary visiting Mecca to perform the Umra (an unscheduled, lesser pilgrimage), noticed a man fast asleep against the wall of the Great Mosque. It was in the middle of the day and quite a few people were busily scurrying around on their way to luncheon and the inevitable siesta. The visitor noticed that the sleeping person was oblivious to all the noise and hubbub around him. "Who might he be?" asked the dignitary of his guide. The latter answered, "Why, this is our ruler." The visitor was speechless. When he opened his mouth again, he uttered the above sentiment in Arabic—the language of the Quran and of Muslim, non-Arab, intellectuals even today.

Many is the time when I have told friends, invoking my wife's testimony, "My conscience is so clear that I sleep extremely well." Facetiousness aside, we could express this quotation in a less literal or elaborate way by saying, "The just feel secure and therefore sleep well," or "Easy lies the head of the just for he (or she) feels secure," or if you will, "Justice is the pillow of composure."

كَيْفَمَا تَكُونُوا يُوَلَّ عَلَيْكُمْ

"Howsoever ye are, so shall your rulers be"

This is attributed to Prophet Muhammad himself. Analyzed today, this precept comes amazingly close to urging the people to make sure whom they vote to office! In other words, if you are good, your officials shall be good; if you are bad, so shall your people in authority be. To me, this wise saying explained in the modern venacular, is enjoining the people to "get up and vote, otherwise, don't complain about the results." Islam and Arab tribal norms acknowledge the wisdom of carefully choosing who shall govern a people. The leader is the pinnacle of the pyramid whose base is the people, but which takes in local chieftains who, in turn, agree on one of their peers to become paramount.

*"Money and children are the adornment
of life on earth"*

This Quranic quotation reflects not only divine wisdom, but also the "pragmatic" sublime outlook on human values. Learned Muslims would point out the order of precedence between money and children. They tell you that money was mentioned before children not because God wants us to value wealth above children, but because He knows that without money we could not take adequate care of our children.

"Paradise is under the feet of mothers"

The concept of Paradise in Islam was rendered with exquisite detail, enumerating the noble pleasures and enviable comforts which will be enjoyed by mortals who qualify for such an ultimate reward. The inference from this quotation from the Prophet of Islam is that by honoring our mothers we score a virtue in the ledger of God's Kingdom. Another possible explanation is that the mothers, by toiling so ceaselessly for the proper upbringing and the well-being of their children, are considered as good as having set foot in Paradise.

 We know that honoring one's parents is one of the Ten Commandments. This filial obligation is also found in Islamic teachings. What is doubly significant in this connection, however, is that mothers are singled out by Prophet Muhammad in this ennobling reference. The Muslim Prophet, himself orphaned at a tender age, realized (long before such various movements as the Woman's Liberation) the role of woman in the family, particularly in raising and guiding children.

*"The best among you are those who are
best to their womenfolk"*

The early followers of Prophet Muhammad were
constantly asking him questions concerning their
daily lives, family, children, honesty and similar
preoccupations. Second to the revelations in the Holy
Quran, the Prophet's utterances on various topics—
whether in response to direct questions or as simple
observations—are the well illuminated landmarks
along the path of the believer.

In this context, the above quotation emphasizes Islam's respect for women and, in fact, elevates the man
who treats his womenfolk well, above him who is not
so gentle or respectful to them. It is noteworthy that
what is meant by "womenfolk" here is not only the
plural of a "woman" or a "wife," but also all other
female dependents on the male head of a family. The
term "hareem," or harem, is one of the most misunder-
stood expressions in the English language. It does not
mean mistresses or concubines. In Arabic, it reflects
the Muslim concept of the females of a household such
as mothers, daughters, sisters, as well as wives. In
other words the "hareem" of the household embraces
those females the protection of whom and the respect
for whom are incumbent on the man.

"Some suspicions are sinful"

The teachings of Islam as revealed to Prophet Muhammad, and conveyed by him to his people, contain many exhortations to those nomads who would follow him. The people of the desert before Islam were fierce warriors whose sport was raiding by one tribe of another. Life in that vast ungenerous terrain was very difficult, giving rise in the character of the Arabian person to several almost instinctive traits. One such was suspicion. We can see how survival dictated that the beduin be at once generous (to those who lose their way and seek shelter), chivalrous (toward those who seek help), and suspicious (of strangers who seem secretive or who do not clarify their mission or purpose). But, as we know, we sometimes jump needlessly to quick and wrong conclusions about a person or a deed. Hence the English saying, "Think the worst and you won't be disappointed." This reference in the holy book of Islam to "some" suspicions being sinful sounds like a direct appeal to those overly suspicious people of the harsh desert to lessen their mistrust of others. Who doesn't remember "Judge not, lest ye be judged?" Or, in the modern vernacular, "Give him the benefit of the doubt?"

اَتَّقِ شَرَّ مَنْ أَحْسَنْتَ إِلَيْهِ

*"Beware of the evil from the recipient
of your charity"*

This warning is another one of those values remembered and repeated even by Muslim children and, in fact, framed and hung in offices and homes for all to see.

It should not be understood that this advice contradicts the previous question about the sinfulness of *some* suspicions. It is, rather, a reminder of the inconsistencies of life on this earth as lived by humans who are an admixture of good and evil. We realize, however, that only the ungrateful reward charity with an evil deed. This is such a familiar blemish on human behavior that we find a comparable reference to such a situation even in some modern expressions in the English language, such as "Don't bite the hand that feeds you." After a friend disappoints you with his ingratitude, you are likely to say, "Well! After all I've done for him! I should know better next time." And this is precisely the message of this quotation: *Just be careful whom you shower with favors.*

"How could you enslave people whose mothers gave birth to them free?"

This rhetorical question is attributed to the second Caliph (successor to Prophet Muhammad) Omar ibn al-Khattab, known for his integrity, justice and compassion. Omar was prompted to exclaim with this expression of indignation, while obviously imbued with the concept of the equality of the faithful as emphasized by Islam.

The Caliph Omar, by the way, lived more than twelve hundred years before Abraham Lincoln!

"Contentment is an inexhaustible treasure"

When we say in English "Half a loaf is better than no bread," we are urging contentment on the person who, without the half a loaf, might be on his way to starvation.

Contrary to the interpretation by some that this Islamic quotation inspires an attitude of "do nothing" or "why bother?", it certainly teaches us the virtue of patience when we, for one reason or another, do not get *all* we want. It seems to recommend that we refrain from feeling fatally depressed when things go wrong for, after all, there's always tomorrow, and tomorrow, and tomorrow!

"Work for this world as though you will live forever: and prepare for the hereafter as though you are dying tomorrow"

If I were asked to suggest one Muslim code of daily behavior to be followed, I would choose this one for its simplicity and universal applicability. Islam urged upon its followers what, in this day and age of over-simplification, may be expressed as "Time and Place For Everything."

Reflections and Comments on Life

خَبِّي قِرْشَك الأبيض ليومك الأسود

"Save your bright coin for your dark day"

 This advice here is similar to the English saying, "Waste Not, Want Not."

سبحان الله بيعطي جوز اللي بلا سنين وبيعطي حلق اللي بلا ودان

"Strange is God's wisdom! He gives walnuts to the toothless, and earrings to the earless"

One is likely to say this out of envy. For instance, if you come across someone who does not do anything good with his or her wealth, especially someone you might consider *nouveau riche,* you might express surprise, mixed perhaps with a touch of envy, at that person's "misplaced," or unmerited, fortune!

Not unlike this image describing a seeming contradiction in a given situation is yet another Arabic saying:

"*The cobbler is barefoot and the weaver is naked*"

Such expressions are fitting to describe, say, a dishevelled beautician or a sloppy fashion designer.

In Egypt particularly they say, in such a situation:

"*The carpenter's door is rickety*"

"What is written can be judged from its title"

This is the literal translation. However, the word for "title" is also used for "address" and by inference, for "introduction." This makes a lot of sense as a general rule, for one can usually get the tone of the letter from the way it is addressed (especially in Arabic where title and honorifics still abound), or from its opening sentences. The type and spirit of the message one receives can also be discerned by knowing its nature and who the sender is: a close friend, junk mail, a bill, an invitation, etc., etc.

The thrust of this quotation is that a smart person can guess what the message is even without reading it all.

A similar notion is embodied in the Arabic popular saying:

"If rain were coming, we would see clouds"

This saying derives directly from climes with distinct seasons such as the Mediterranean type of climate, which prevails also in Florida, California and parts of Australia. In such places overcast skies generally mean rain is coming.

Within this context, if you say to an Arab who is down and out that his condition will soon improve, he might, in the absence of any sudden indication to support your cheery message, reply "Thanks, pal, but if rain were coming we would see clouds!" Remember that rain is a blessing in arid areas. (This quotation appears quite contradictory to many Westerners in climatic environments such as England. The sky could be completely overcast yet not one drop of rain would fall!)

If the people of a country are influenced by its climate, then it seems strange that the Mediterranean people are often regarded as unpredictable, whereas the British, for instance, are known as solid, down to earth people of great composure and clarity. The explanation, perhaps, lies in the fact that *because* of the unpredictability of the British weather, those calm people must be prepared for all eventualities!

"Since I am drowning, why should I fear getting wet?"

This is one of the Arabic ways of saying "Things Couldn't Get Worse!"

The Egyptians express the same sentiment colloquially, but also graphically, when they say:

"When hit on his blind eye, he said it's no good, anyway"

This is typical of the Egyptian character, especially in the rural areas where a combination of religious fatalism, native pragmatism and infinite patience mitigate against losing one's temper too quickly. Some analysts, or sociobiologists may call this indolence or submissiveness, but that would be a superficial characterization.

أَلْقَاهُ فِي الْيَمِّ مَكْتُوفًا وَقَالَ لَهُ

إِيَّاكَ إِيَّاكَ أَنْ تَبْتَلَّ بِالْمَاءِ

"He tied him up then flung him into the ocean,
warning him never, never, to get wet"

This quotation is used to illustrate an impossible situtation. The ingredients of the saying spell a predicament with no easy way out. It's like a mother permitting her child to jump into a pool on one condition: "Don't get wet."

Another Arabic imagery of a predicament is found in a popular injunction often quoted by Arabs to make a point of unrealism. It is as one person might say to another who had just asked for some bread:

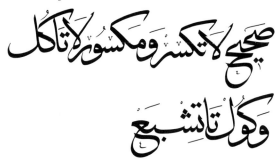

"Whole loaves do not break; broken pieces do not eat; but consume all you can!"

وَمَا الْمَرْءُ إِلَّا كَالشِّهَابِ وَضَوْئِهِ

يَحُورُ رَمَادًا بَعْدَ إِذْ هُوَ سَاطِعُ

"How like a shooting star and its quick flashes
man's life doth seem: once bright, then ashes."

 The preceding is a touching Arabic
quotation reflecting our utter helpless-
ness in the face of tragedy. I remembered it on the occasion of the death of
those three brave astronauts who per-
ished in the fire which raged in the
space vehicle while preparing for a
simulated first Apollo Mission to the
Moon.

الشورى البشرية والعلاقات الإنسانية

Human Relations and Behavior

*"Your faith is judged by your
treatment of others"*

This Arabic quotation is so succinct (two words) that it would be almost impossible to match its brevity in English. The intent of the saying, which is often quoted by Arabs, Christian as well as Muslim or Jewish, is to indicate that you cannot claim to be a person of piety or religious goodness by simply going to your place of worship or reciting prescribed prayers. Your goodness would be evident in the way you treat, or deal with, others.

"The close ones have prior claim on your favor"

This is reminiscent of "Charity begins at home." The idea is still generally held by Arabs and Muslims in their daily practices and perceptions, not excluding even their political life. Brotherhood and kinship continue to be held up high as imperative criteria of good, praiseworthy behavior. In this sense, they do not condone such a questioning sentiment one hears in other societies as "Am I my brother's keeper?!" A true Muslim or Arab would immediately reply: "Of course I am my brother's keeper if he is genuinely in need of my help and succor." In fact, those who have experienced life in Arab and Muslim lands would perhaps remember how mutual help among a group of relatives or even friends has been likened to the social security system of the West. What Muslim charitable acts lack in computerization or publicity, they more than make up in the pleasure of giving and the solace in receiving.

The reader will, I'm sure, recall several such attitudes, teachings and practices in Christianity before religious zeal in some countries of the Western world began to wane as a major influence on our daily lives.

 Talking about good deeds, favors or charities, an Arabic quotation would be very apt in this regard. It is:

"The giver of charity should not mention it; and the receiver should not forget it"

Mention has already been made of how quotations such as these apply even to the political field. A case in point is the western habit of expecting, if not demanding in advance, almost instant reward, acknowledgement or gratitude from the party receiving a good deed, favor or charity. We do not fail to ask "What's in it for me?", or "What have you done for me lately?", or "There is nothing for nothing," not to forget the famous "Quid pro quo."

When I was in the US government service, I used to cringe whenever I read the publicity campaign accompanying the sacks of flour donated "by the American people" to the inhabitants of such and such a country in temporary or chronic distress. My discomfiture was certainly not caused by the marvelous act of charity attributed to the American people. Rather, what bothered and embarrassed me was the planned promotional photography campaign by the United States Information Service to publicize the charity of the United States. One prominent local official attending the unloading of such a "floury" gift said to me, "Now, your people would want me to make a long speech! I am tempted to observe that the poor photographers and publicists should be urged to rest and relax since at least one picture was made of each sack showing the US flag on the sleeve of the giver."

Thank goodness that, as I understand it, USIA has become more prudent and diplomatic.

"Paradise without people is not worth setting foot in"

Arabs are impulsive socializers. They are not the sullen, taciturn introverts depicted so often by Western films, magazines and newspapers. Actually the oft cited generosity of the Arabs stems directly from their instinctive love of company, of people to talk to, and of guests to visit and share a meal or an event. In Arab-Muslim society it is not only misery which likes company but, more importantly, happiness also— whether it is already present or can be brought about.

مَنْ شَافَ مصِيبَةَ غَيْرَهُ
هَانَتْ عَلَيهِ مصِيبَتُهُ

"He who sees the calamity of another
finds his bearable"

This could be rendered as Troubles Shared Are Less Painful. In fact, the Arabic quotation does not make it necessary that you pool your misery with that of another person. It does mean that, if you have an affliction, a handicap or an unpleasant experience, you would tend to reflect on how "comparatively lucky" you are if you saw another person in similar or more onerous circumstances.

Such an expression is used to give hope and consolation to less fortunate persons who might, otherwise, feel constantly sorry for themselves.

"The camel limped because of his lip"

In other words, the camel gave the wrong cause for his lameness. He attributed his limp to a totally irrelevant reason, namely his split upper lip. This is like the person who lisped badly yet, nevertheless, applied for the position of a broadcaster at the local station. The story has it that when a friend asked him why he was not accepted for the job by the station director, the applicant replied, still lisping, "Becauth I theemed tho thmall!!"

"The bald woman takes pride
in her cousin's hair"

Just like a pauper saying, "The Rockefellers and I have millions of dollars!"

أَجَا يَكَحِّلْهَا عَمَاهَا

"He came to beautify the eye; instead,
he poked it out"

This is said when you ask someone to repair or improve something that is of value to you and, instead of doing that, he breaks or damages the item. The lesson to be drawn from this quotation could very well be that we should exercise great care when we seek help — always ask the professional.

إِسْأَلْ مُجَرِّب وَلَا تْسَأَلْ حَكِيم

"Ask an experienced person, rather than a sage"

This quotation also urges reliance on professionalism, supported by experience, as a recourse for solutions. Quite often it proves more beneficial to consult an experienced man rather than a " wise " man.

"Press not your hand so tightly to your chest, nor stretch it out so open that you might come to bemoan your extravagance as misfortune"

The English interpretation is but an attempt to convey the sense of this magnificent quotation from the Quran. In the original Arabic the verse is so beautifully measured and so delicately balanced that it fits like a glove on the "hand." It seeks to teach us to avoid either of the two extremes: stinginess and squandering. I have always considered this wise counsel as the essence of sound economy, individual or national.

"Every steed is permitted one stumble"

The Arabs are likely to use this quotation when a smart person makes a serious mistake, or commits an act usually unworthy of him or her. In a case like this, and by way of an apologia, an Arab would make the above statement by which at least two points are underscored: a blunder has in fact been made; and such a blunder is so unusual from a person so highly esteemed that it is akin to an exceptional stumble by a matchless steed, and therefore is forgivable.

Commenting on the fuss made of such a blunder or *faux pas* by an otherwise very clever person, an Arab might say:

غَلْطَةُ الشَّاطِرِ بِأَلْفِ غَلْطَة

"The mistake of the smart is magnified a thousandfold"

If an Arab does not genuinely support or like a certain group of officials, or teachers, for instance, and you ask for his or her opinion of that group, don't be surprised when the reply comes out succinctly as "When Horses are Scarce. . . . !" The full quotation is:

"When horses are scarce, you saddle dogs!"

Can't you just hear such imagery being voiced during, say, an electioneering campaign?!

Kinship, Friendship and Neighborliness are manifested much more openly by the Arabs and Muslims than by Westerners. Quotations testifying to this factual statement are innumerable. Suffice it to illustrate a few samples in the area of human relations:

"You may acquire a brother not of your blood"

When you get to know someone so well and develop with him a closeness and trust normally perceived to develop between two brothers, while that person is not even a blood relative, you are said to have acquired a brother not of your blood. This concept is not totally strange to such communities, societies or clubs where fellow members are known to hail each other as "Brother."

"Cherish your brother, for he who is brotherless
is like a warrior without weapons"

"One's cousin, you should also know, is like a
wing to a falcon. Can falcons fly without wings?"

"Rather a close neighbor than a distant brother"

In human relationships it is not rare for two friends
and relatives to become estranged from each other. In
such a situation magnanimity requires one to wish for
the other person's wellbeing as well as his absence.
Thus an Arab would say of his erstwhile friend:

الله يِسْعِـدْهُ وَيِبْـعِـدْهُ

"May God keep him happy but distant"

صَدِيقُكَ مَنْ صَدَقَكَ لَا مَنْ صَدَّقَكَ

"Your friend is he who tells you the truth,
not he who agrees with everything you say"

This is one particular saying which I heard the late
King Faisal of Saudi Arabia use so frequently with
American high officials and diplomats every time
they wondered about his criticism of U.S. policies.

الجَارُ قَبْلَ الدَّارِ
وَالرَّفِيقُ أَوَّلاً ثُمَّ الطَّرِيقُ

*"Choose the neighbor before the house and
the companion before the journey"*

Having enumerated the above examples, I must hasten to remark that, as with life itself, such perceptions or codes of behavior have their own pragmatic adjustments and variations even, or especially, among the Arabs who have long suffered a mistaken reputation of being unpragmatic. Such variations on certain of the above themes are:

أَنَا وَأَخِي عَلَى ابْنِ عَمِّي
وَأَنَا وَابْنُ عَمِّي عَلَى الْغَرِيبِ

*"My brother and I against my cousin;
my cousin and I against the stranger"*

احْذَرْ عَدُوَّكَ مَرَّةً
وَاحْذَرْ صَدِيقَكَ الْفَ مَرَّةً
فَلَرُبَّمَا انْقَلَبَ الصَّدِيقُ
فَصَارَ أَعْلَمَ بِالْمَضَرَّةِ

*"Be careful of your enemy once
and of your friend a thousand times"
"For should your friend cease to be true
he'd be more able to hurt you"*

In a society whose favorite sport was constant raiding, before Islam tempered the beduin's zeal for such adventures and before King Abdel Aziz unified what came to be known as Saudi Arabia and ended the traditional incursions by the tribes into each other's territory, loyalties tended to be precarious. Your friend today might be swayed away from you into alliance with your enemy. Hence this practical advice about staying wary of the potential danger to you from friend as well as foe.

We all know that "two minds are better than one," i.e. that it is always useful to consult and seek the advice of experts and trusted friends. The Arabs have ranked wise counsel even above personal bravery which they had in abundant measure. Indeed, even in the Quran — the holy book of Islam — mutual counsel is a specific injunction required of the faithful. It is called (Shoura) and the English approximation would be concensus "collective opinion" resulting from wide and deep consultation among the group. Each individual would offer his opinion (rai) in the process of shoura. The consensus would then be held higher than sheer bravery or adventurism. Hence the Arabic quotation:

الرَّأْيُ قَبْلَ شَجَاعَةِ الشُّجْعَانِ
هُوَ أَوَّلُ وَهِــــىَ الْمَحَلُّ الثَّانِي

"Wise counsel should be your first choice, the second should be bravery"

Another way of putting it in English could be: "First seek counsel, then be brave."

The Arabs and Muslims I know have no liking for
meekness if it is synonymous with servility. To them,
modesty—the antithesis of haughtiness—is a virtue,
but not the kind of meekness which is often misunder-
stood, and malpracticed, by "literal" Christians.

 Practically every Arab high school student has memorized a famous line of
poetry which says:

*"The servile brooks humiliation
just as a corpse feels no pain"*

The following quotation is very frequently dangled as proof positive that the Arabs see relationships in only black and white colors—no gray shades. When they like you, it is said, they idolize you; when they dislike you, they hate your guts! To some extent this is true, but is it not also true, though perhaps manifested differently, with the "sophisticated" Europeans? Has not this human "frailty" been fully exercised during several wars when we conveniently sought to forge friendships and alliances on the one hand, and build up national ire against adversaries and enemies on the other? Be that as it may, the telling Arabic quotation is:

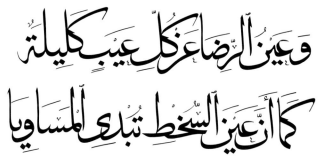

"Contented eyes to all the faults are blind;
but eyes displeased will only weakness find"

Those who understand and appreciate the eloquence and near majesty of this Arabic quotation will sympathize with me for pouring it into a classical mold.

40

*"But for broken pottery, the kilns
would go broke"*

This is said usually to put at ease a guest who
accidentally breaks something of value to you and
pours out profuse apologies. Out of politeness, the
host or hostess must use some kind of a consoling
remark, though the temptation may be almost irresist-
ible to gnash his or her teeth and hiss, "How Clumsy
You Are!!"

Arabic is full of expressions of niceties which are used
on a multitude of occasions for the specific purpose of
putting a friend or acquaintance at ease. As an alterna-
tive to the above quotation, an Arab might simply say:

اِنْكَسَرَ ٱلشَّرّ

"Evil has been broken"

It is as though you are thanking your guest for having
done you the favor of dispelling evil (the evil eye,
envy) by breaking something of value. It can readily
be seen that this Arab outlook is the exact opposite of
the superstition in the West, which holds that to break
a mirror brings one seven years of bad luck.

41

"Those with brains are at rest"

You can say this as a polite way of showing your displeasure with certain types of people. The implication is that the world must be full of idiots because the brainy, clever ones are all dead, hence "at rest." Notice that the person using this expression never seems to include himself or herself among those "at rest!"

"A sharp tongue cuts deeper than a sword"

The Arabs have always attached great importance to words, hence their extra sensitivity to compliments, insults or indifference. This fact is not heeded adequately by key Western persons or organizations when they seek to establish good relations with the Arab people. The vast gulf in attitudes towards the spoken word (between the Arabs and the uninitiated Westerners) becomes evident, and almost natural, when we remember the English nursery rhyme with which Anglo-Saxon children grow up: namely, "Sticks and stones may break my bones, but words will never hurt me."

"Nothing scratches your skin like your own nails"

In other words, you are the one to pinpoint the location of the "itch" and therefore the most qualified to "scratch" it satisfactorily and quickly. Attempts by others to "scratch" you end up being a series of trial and error. So, why not "do it yourself?"

Apart from the soundness of the literal meaning of this quotation, it will be noticed that it places emphasis on "centralization." This has for centuries been typical of Third World societies: the almost total absence of the practice of delegating authority to subordinates. I presume that the reason behind this over-centralization is the lack of enough qualified and loyal persons to be entrusted with authority, or — more seriously — the absence of confidence in one's subordinates. The Arabs have been described as too individualistic. This may be true, but this quality is being gradually balanced by the acquisition of modern techniques and principles of management. It used to be a truism that from a group of four Arabs, you got six opinions. Nowadays, if you have four Arab participants in a discussion, you may come out with only three views. Progress indeed!

As a corollary, a metaphorical expression in Arabic, suggesting ingratiation through praise and tailored compliments, is "Scratch him where he itches." While Westerners do not recommend "scratching" it is well known that politicians often "butter up" or "soap up" an influential person or group, especially in the course of electioneering. In this effort if a different person or group is benefiting accidentally, an Arab might say:

"For the sake of roses, brambles get watered"

The application of this quotation is quite diverse. Generally speaking, it means that we often have to put up with hardships, nuisances and discomforts in order to get the satisfaction of reaching our goal. For instance, you would be less than wise to antagonize the mother of the girl you wish to cultivate. In this case, you should rather pay attention to the "bramble" while praising the "rose!"

This quotation also applies equally to the world of business. For instance, you sometimes have to persuade junior officials of your point of view in order to get to the company president or key person in whose hands lies the decision for the consummation of the deal or the awarding of a sizable contract.

"Blame is commensurate with fondness"

Many people are hypersensitive to criticism even from close relatives or friends. When a person you love or are fond of gives you the impression that you are remonstrating too much with him or her, the above quotation should serve as your best retort. For, after all, if you did not care about that person, you would not bother to blame, or pick a bone, with him or her for, say, not writing to you for a long time, or for not including you in the celebration of a happy event.

Put in another way, the person resenting such fond criticism should remember the famous American film actress-humorist Mae West, who said "I'd rather be looked over than overlooked!"

This extra sensitivity is found in old, proud persons or nations as well as in the very young. The Arabs are no exception among the venerable vulnerable any more than the Americans are among the dauntless, faultless young!

The times are innumerable when I had to use this quotation to pacify both sides in a discussion or in the wake of an editorial in the American or Arab press critical of the policy of the other side. When I was assigned to Saudi Arabia, some twenty-five years ago, as the first Director of Public Affairs at the U.S. Embassy, I undertook a training course involving discussions on the background of that country and its people. I recall distinctly the impression that several officials in the U.S. Government considered then Crown Prince Faisal as "America's enemy number one" in the Middle East. When, incredulously, I would ask "Why?", the simplistic reply would be, "Because he doesn't go along with — indeed, he criticizes — our policy in that area!!"

How ironic it must have seemed that when Faisal was assassinated his death was lamented in the West as the demise of our best, and most consistent, friend in the area. To me, this reversal in attitude was a sign of our maturity of judgment. The man himself had not changed. He was, until his death, a sincere but not unquestioning friend. We, however, learned to differentiate between the straight-from-the-shoulder counseling of a true friend and the abject, syrupy flattery of a fawning lackey.

"Spoil a dog but not a man"

The reader will quickly grasp the implied reference to the ungratefulness of human beings. The Arabic expression admits that you could spoil a dog with food and attention all you like. But if you were to lessen your "gifts" or even stop them completely, your dog will not bite you. By contrast, if the same situation happens with a person to whom you had shown kindness or generosity, then stopped or even reduced your gift, you will very likely acquire an instant detractor, if not an enemy. In this case we would say that your human friend took you for granted, an action which is unknown to ever-loyal dogs.

 Another human weakness is unfolded in yet another Arabic expression using the dog as the central figure. It says:

"Keep your dog hungry, it will follow you"

The intention is not that you should *starve* your dog, but keep it a little hungry. In other words, as some would say in the world of business and commerce, "Never give the customer all he wants."

In human relationship, it means: Keep the other person coming to you, seeking your help or favor.

A few intriguing sayings which are especially popular in Egypt indicate, as no psychological treatise could, the flexibility which those down-to-earth Egyptian people possess in abundance. In this day and age, the following saying might prove very popular with politicians and negotiators of all races:

إِنْ كَانَ لَكَ عِنْدَ الْكَلْبِ حَاجَةٌ
قُلْ لَهُ يَا سَيِّدِي

"If you need something badly from even a dog, call him 'Sir'"

Now, lest this Egyptian saying appear to advocate excessive servility, another seems to draw a line beyond which a supplicant should not go. It is phrased in an interrogative and surprised vein:

"You want my charity and my obeisance too?!"

As can be seen, this is a valid criticism of a person who badly wants a favor, or charity, from you; yet, instead of his addressing you respectfully or at least cordially, he insists that you bow to him while he condescends to accept!

Such an arrogant charity seeker is immortalized in one Arabic verse which differentiates between two categories of recipients of generous favors — the decent and the mean:

"Generosity captivates the decent,
but antagonizes the mean"

Still in the field of human relations we learn in the Arabic vernacular:

الإيد اللّي ماتقدرش عليها بوسها وادعي عليها بالكسر

"When you cannot withstand the upper hand, kiss it and wish it broken!"

Does this teach hypocrisy or simulation? Maybe. It certainly taught many ancient peoples who practiced the intent of this quotation a necessary lesson for survival. Modern societies are not immune to this formula of bending with the storm (while cursing it?!). We all remember, of course, "If you can't beat them, join them."

An apt Arabic quotation preaching non-involvement or firmly putting a stop to an unpleasant situation goes like this:

"Close shut the door that brings the draft"

Another piece of advice which, in a wicked world, might smack of isolationism is the Arabic saying:

"Turn away from evil and rejoice"

The English expression "to start on the wrong foot" indicates that failure is the result of such a start. In Arabic there are several sayings which predict doom or at least what might be known in the vernacular as a non-starter. One such Arabic expression is:

"On his first raid he broke his weapon"

This saying is taken from the times when the tribes of the desert indulged in raids against one another for booty and supremacy. If a warrior who was naive or unseasoned was defeated on his "maiden raid," he was said to have broken his weapon (actually, "stick" or "club" in Arabic) at first dash. The same would be said of a new leader who starts out his term, or rule, with an unpopular act like raising taxes, restricting freedoms or firing from office decent, respectable people who happen to have many followers.

Similarly, if a young person goes for an interview with a prospective employer and, instead of being polite, alert and knowledgeable, begins by denigrating the firm, its policies or its products, that person would be said to have "broken his weapon on the first raid."

In a more literary vein, such an unfortunate first step is likened to a blasphemous opening of a poem!

"The start of the poem is blasphemy"

Let me end this chapter with a few Arabic quotable quotes which need a minimum of explanation or none at all.

"Better fame than fortune"

"An hour's pain is better than constant suffering"

Said to encourage visiting the dentist?!

لاَقِنِي وَلاَ تَغَدِّينِي

"I'd rather be well received than well fed"

In Tunisia they have a saying in this self-respecting sense. It is:

شِدِّ خُبْزَتَكَ وَاطْلِقْ عَبَسْتَكَ

"Take back your bread but release your frown"

Obviously such dignified sentiments come more easily to the opulent and less hungry. In a situation where food is spread before a group of people who are truly hungry, one should not expect intellectual exchanges between mouthfuls. In fact you might even hear someone murmuring:

عِنْدَ الْبُطُونِ ضَاعَتِ الْعُقُولُ

"Busy stomachs, absent minds"

"Feed the mouth, close the eyes"

This is said in cases where you might gain somebody's cooperation, or connivance, by inviting him to a sumptuous dinner or slipping him something worth his silence!

On the other hand there are persons who would not be satisfied with just a meal or a gift. Of such a person it would be said, especially in Egypt and western Saudi Arabia:

"Give him your finger, he'd demand your arm"

Similar to "Give him an inch, he'd take a mile."

"Less visits, more welcome"

A somewhat similar thought is found in the English saying "Familiarity Breeds Contempt."

"The absent has his excuse with him"

In other words, give the absent person the benefit of the doubt. Don't ascribe ulterior motives to his or her absence, say, from a meeting or dinner.

"Follow the burglar up to the door"

The meaning is that only by doing so would you discover whether the other person is really a burglar, and only after he goes inside the place and starts burglarizing.

Should that person be, in fact, a burglar and he gains easy access to the house or shop because the door is open or unlocked, you might be tempted (unless you are a police officer) to shake your head and say almost sympathetically with the burglar:

"Unattended wealth teaches thievery"

"No right is lost if its claimant is determined"

This is a truism known to lawyers and judges alike. The statute of limitations, however, implies that the claimant of that lost right has neglected or abandoned it for a specific time during which he was too bored or disinterested to enforce it. In this case one could say that such a person, or nation for that matter, has almost asked to lose that right!

Western bureaucracy has developed a fine chain of command as basic to any establishment, military or civilian. Reference has already been made to the Arab's historic over-centralization of authority in tribal societies. Islam brought with it a certain administrative code which worked exceedingly well for the Muslim Empire, which within one century spread from the Atlantic Ocean to the borders of China. The faithful were enjoined to obey "God, His messenger and those in authority among you." The chain of command ensured that the local governor reported to his regional boss, who in turn reported to the ruler in the central capital. It is perhaps out of this clearer delineation of authority in the Muslim hierarchy that one or two golden rules emerged. One is:

"When you don't command obedience, don't issue orders"

Another dictum is:

*"If you want to be obeyed,
demand what is possible"*

In this sense the modern expression might be " Be reasonable , " even though some bosses have been known to put a large plaque on their desks urging their subordinates and associates to "Be reasonable: do it my way!"

What do you do when your friend or acquaintance suffers a misfortune which you have luckily been spared: death in the family, great loss of capital, a heavy fine, etc., etc.? Instinctively, you try to console your friend with appropriate expressions of sympathy and encouragement. However, there is an unmarked border which you should not cross in such a situation. It is the dividing line between the soothing word and the irritating, verbal bandage. For instance, if you are not in a position to save your friend's financial embarrassment by giving him a loan, don't try to hypnotize him with rosy pictures of the future and how "it could be worse!" For if you do and your friend is conversant with Arabic, he might give you a funny look while saying: "It's all very well for you to say that because:

"Receiving the lashes is not the same as counting them"

By this your friend means that he is the one who is being lynched, or whipped, by his misfortune, whereas you are just a bystander counting the painful lashes which he is receiving. So how could you be so "unfeeling" as to suggest that things could be worse?!

Family Relationships, Social Norms

مَا أَعَزُّ مِنَ الْوَلَدِ إِلَّا وَلَدُ الْوَلَدِ

*"No one is dearer than the child
save the grandchild"*

Apart from the general acceptability of this sentiment among humans, it has been so often used as a further appeal to a grandparent to "baby sit" when the parents of a child want to go out. Or when, say, the grandmother feels like giving advice to the child's mother about "the health and welfare of my grandchild."

*"Once your son grows up,
treat him as a brother"*

This injunction is known to apply equally to the mother-daughter relationship. However, in certain societies where parental attachments are very strong, where worldly wisdom is frequently considered synonymous with "age" and grey hair, this advice is easier said than done. Such reluctance on the parent's part to let go of a son or daugher at a given age to try the wings independently is shunned by many Westerns as "over-protectionism." A mother who hovers over a mature son who happens to be visiting his parental home is often referred to, with a mixture of amusement and derision, as behaving like a "Jewish mother"; indeed an "Arab mother" would be equally apt in the circumstances. In that kind of society where parents address their children, even grown-up sons and daughters, as "love of my heart," "light of my eyes" or "my life" and so on, it is not easy, for a mother especially, to break away from that habit or attitude.

In the West the opposite stance is the accepted norm. Children are encouraged at a very early age to "stand on your own two feet." I still remember how I was speechless with incredulity when I was told that the only two children, ages seven and five, of an English couple were being sent away to a boarding school! To the person who has not been exposed to this semi-Spartan upbringing, such early relinquishment of parental attachment, not to say love and joy of attentiveness, comes dangerously close to seeming callous.

In family relations where devotedness is not reciprocated—and this usually is manifest during the children's adolescence and the attendant rebelliousness—a doting parent not from an Anglo-Saxon background might be heard to say plaintively:

"*My heart bleeds for my child, but my child's heart is made of stone*"

*"The male child is two-thirds like
his maternal uncle"*

This is a time-honored belief among the Arabs. In the
Arabian Peninsula, even to this day, a person's pride
in the mother's family tree is almost as great as in the
father's. Since a person's family name is derived from
the father, and is, therefore, readily known, one's
maternal genealogy is, on the other hand, the first topic
raised when inquiring about a person newly intro-
duced. "Who are his maternal uncles?" is often question number one.

Lest the female segment of society feel bypassed, the
Arabs have balanced the picture by claiming that the
female child takes after one of her father's sisters, if not
after her mother.

The readers are invited to put these two ancient beliefs
to the test, starting with their own families. Let me
know what the results are!

Many are the Arabic sayings on marriage: who, when, why; a cousin or relative before a stranger; marrying a person of good breeding, and so on. Marriages based solely on monetary gain soon evoke the following saying, with the word 'monkey' used to indicate a less-than-attractive spouse:

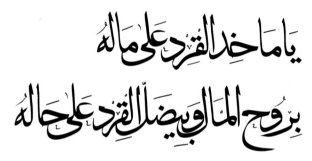

"Before you marry a monkey for the money, remember that the monkey might outlive its wealth"

 Mothers-in-law are traditionally, and in many divergent societies, subjected to an inordinate amount of lampooning. We have often heard the husband railing, to his wife or circle of male friends, at his mother-in-law. Well, here is one quotation where a mother-in-law is side-swiping her son's wife who has displeased her and who, therefore, needs some chiding, albeit indirectly!

"I'm talking to you, neighbor, so that my daughter-in-law can hear"

The idea is, at least procedurally, close to the English quotation, "Strike one to frighten another."

When "Johnny can do no wrong," according to his mother at least, the Arabs express this situation in a picturesque way, by saying:

"A monkey, in his mother's eye, is a gazelle"

Finally, to end this chapter on a very attractive concept revolving around the parent-child relationship, I should like to treat the reader to a quotation which might evoke the reaction I often expressed quietly: namely, "I wish I had said that!" The quotation on the following page is in fact a response to a single, ordinary question asked of a father.

سُئِلَ حَكِيمٌ أَيُّ أَوْلَادِكَ أَحَبُّ إِلَيْكَ

فَأَجَابَ صَغِيرُهُمْ حَتَّى يَكْبَرَ

وَسَقِيمُهُمْ حَتَّى يَبْرَأَ

وَغَائِبُهُمْ حَتَّى يَعُودَ

"A wise man was asked 'Which of your
children is your favorite?' The wise man
replied: 'The young one until he grows up,
the sick one until he recovers
and the absent one until he returns.'"

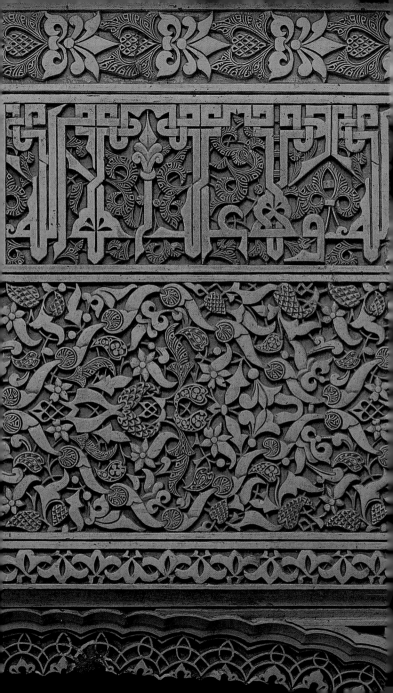

الدبلوماسية

Diplomacy

Students of Arab and Islamic history will tell you that, in their heyday, Arab governments attained a very high level of sophistication in the field of diplomatic relations: exchange of notes, dispatching of emissaries, political pronouncements and so on. For the specific purpose of this book it is enough to list a few quotations which are still current. They are, in my opinion, the residual of inherited annals of Arab diplomacy and prescribed behavior.

"Not everything that is known can be told"

While this quotation might displease modern so-called investigative reporters in certain Western countries, especially in the United States, most of Third World countries hold that it is the privilege of those in authority to decide when and what could be released for public consumption. Yet the self-same quotation could be used as a modern diplomat's escape hatch if he finds himself cornered and pressed for an immediate response on a given point. In other words, this Arabic saying could serve as a cover-up for the diplomat's inadequate knowledge of his government's latest policy stand. If the Western diplomat remembers this useful quotation and utters it in enough of a somber, all-wise tone, he or she, in order to score a point positively, must hasten to add, with a knowing look, "but I will urge my government to permit me to convey it (whatever the 'it' detail is) to Your Excellency, but on a strictly confidential basis, of course!"

 In diplomacy the practitioner should never be caught telling an out-and-out lie. Explicable variations on a given element of truth, an occasional stretching of a point which is essentially truthful, may be tolerated. But glaring fabrications or falsehoods would evoke the apt Arabic saying:

"The rope of lies is always too short"

This is like saying in English that the liar will ultimately give himself enough rope to hang himself.

A similar quotation, but in the form of advice, is:

"If you are a habitual liar, you'd better have a good memory"

Diplomacy that resorts to ambiguities in order to escape an impasse, or to buy time, very often reaps a harvest not only of confusion but also of reproach, recrimination and, worse still, bitter enmity. Examples are not difficult to find. An Arabic expression, taken from the practice of sharecropping, says:

"Understanding in the field avoids disputes on the threshing floor"

What is meant by "understanding" here is the amicable arrangements arrived at between two parties as a result of clear stipulations laid down at the outset. These days one needs a battery of legal firms to remove the cobwebs of ambiguity or to uncover the purposeful traps. Hence, the popular advice to "read between the lines" or "read the fine print" in a contract.

Another expression used by the Arabs to indicate a similar situation is:

"What starts with a clear condition ends with satisfaction"

History tells us that in ancient societies it was not uncommon for a ruler to order his emissary beheaded just because the poor soul brought back to his boss an unpleasant response from a distant chief or bad news from a source over which the emissary had no control. Islam frowned upon such earlier practices and decreed instead that:

"The messenger has only to convey"

In other words, a messenger should not indulge in "editorializing" the message or interpreting it voluntarily. This sounds like the genesis of holding the messenger blameless and therefore unpunishable for doing his job. Isn't this development in attitude a prelude to "diplomatic immunity?"

To underscore this presumed innocence on the part of an emissary, or a diplomat, the latter, if he or she senses that the person receiving the message is becoming irritated, could justifiably say something like this:

*"The conveyor of blasphemy
is not himself blasphemous"*

A modern diplomat, with a passion for the American vernacular, might plead "Don't blame me, Sir: I didn't *make* the policy!"

If you ponder the following quotation carefully you will begin to see the connection between shoeing a horse and conducting diplomacy. If you have the tendency to be heavy handed or over-zealous when discussing a topic leading, hopefully, to an amicable arrangement, your Arab friend or observer would attemp to calm you down or pull you back a bit by suggesting:

"Strike once the shoe and once the nail"

Reference to shoe and nail is quite obviously related to the act of shoeing a horse. Unless computerization or mechanization has taken over everything, shoeing a horse involves quite a technique; you don't drive a nail into the horse's hoof through the shoe by constant hammering on the nail. The expert shoe-smith alternates the hammer pressure between the shoe and the nail in order to give both recipients of the blows, not to mention the horse, time to settle down and relax painlessly. Otherwise the shoe might get warped when the same nail is hammered in too deeply.

So it is with diplomacy. You need time for the ideas, notions, suggestions or attitudes to sink in. Besides, "easy does it" is true more often than not.

In our daily pursuits, including diplomatic endeavors, we sometimes confuse the other party by using too much gentility or too tough a stand. The prescribed "happy medium" formula in Arab and Islamic history is:

"*Lenience without weakness and firmness without violence*"

A parallel Arab advice is:

"*Be not so soft as to be squeezed dry, nor so stiff as to be broken*"

During Dr. Henry Kissinger's Shuttle Diplomacy, which a wicked friend called (a slip of the tongue?) "Shuffle" Diplomacy, I quoted to the then U.S. Secretary of State what every Arab student is proud of quoting as the golden rule of Arab-Islamic diplomacy. It is called Sha'rat Muaawiya, that is, Muaawiya's Hair. An explanation is quite in order here as it was for the benefit of Dr. K.

Muaawiya was the founder of the Umayyad dynasty and the first Umayyad caliph (d. 680 A.D.). He had participated in the Islamic conquest of Syria during the rules of Omar and Othman (2nd and 3rd successors, caliphs, respectively, of Prophet Muhammad). Muaawiya opposed the succession of Ali ibn Abi Taleb, the Prophet's cousin and son-in-law, fought him at the battle of Siffeen (657 A.D.) until arbitration was agreed upon. The result was that Muaawiya, through clever maneuvering, we are told, acquired the caliphate and ruled the then Islamic domain with Damascus as his capital.

The diplomatic golden rule attributed to Muaawiya is his saying:

"Should there be but one hair between me and the others, I would not have it cut: for if they slacken it I would pull, and if they pull it I would slacken it some"

This image based on one hair gave the saying its abbreviation: Muaawiya's Hair.

At one point during Dr. Kissinger's Shuttlomacy, when the going was somewhat rough for him, he turned to me and said "Don't you think your Arab friends have not only cut the hair of the caliph you mentioned but have indeed singed his whole beard?!" I rose to Dr. K's habitual bantering, which I enjoyed perhaps as much as he, and assured him that my friends had not yet cut that hair, nor singed the beard. What they were doing, I said, was trying to *trim* the beard, that is to clarify the relationship with him!

Muaawiya's quoted expression is what present-day diplomats like Dr. Kissinger (is there anyone like Dr. K.?!) would mean by using the phrase "keeping up the dialogue."

One of the most apt remarks which a negotiator could use in a pinch, when the opposite number claims, rather deviously, not to understand what is being said, is to treat the "clever one" to an equally clever expression by the famous Lebanese-American writer-philospher, Gibran Kahlil Gibran. It is this expression with which I have chosen to end this chapter. Said Gibran:

"Your claim not to understand me is praise I do not merit and an insult you do not deserve."

Mosque of Ibn Tulun, Cairo, p. *ii*
Dome of the Grand Mosque, Cordoba, p. *xii*
Court of the Lions at the Alhambra, Granada, p. *12*
Ceiling in the Alhambra, Granada, p. *22*
Traditional buildings, old Jeddah, p. *62*
Stucco ornament at the Alhambra, Granada, p. *72*

Produced by Ray Graham & Associates, Inc.
Designers: Michael T. Graham/Missy Lipsett
Calligrapher: M. V. Zakariya
End papers: Don Gyot
Photographer: Robert Emmett Bright

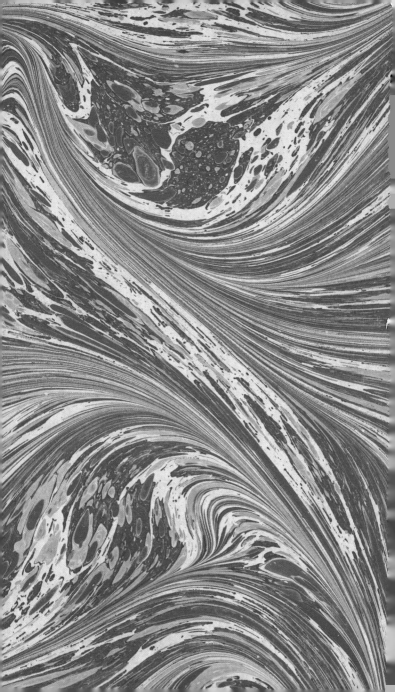